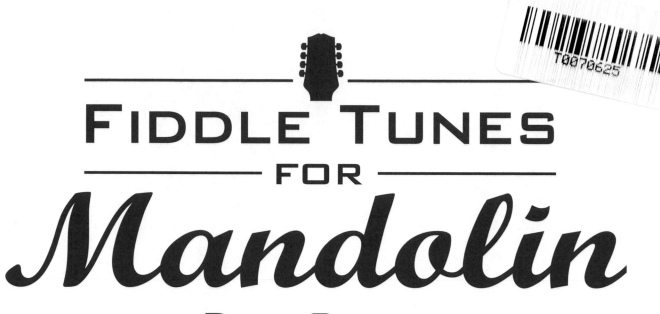

FIDDLE TUNES
FOR
Mandolin

BY DICK SHERIDAN

To access audio visit:
www.halleonard.com/mylibrary

Enter Code
7195-5595-5134-2276

The audio online, although not played on the mandolin, will be especially helpful if you're unfamiliar with a particular piece.
Play along with either the melody or the chords or simply enjoy listening to the songs.

ISBN 978-1-57424-324-6
SAN 683-8022

RM-1 Walnut Mandolin on the cover courtesy of National Reso-Phonic Guitars

Cover by James Creative Group

Copyright © 2015 CENTERSTREAM Publishing, LLC
P.O. Box 17878 - Anaheim Hills, CA 92817

www.centerstream-usa.com

Irvin Rouse, composer of the most recorded fiddle tune in the world the "Orange Blossom Special"

Contents

About The Arranger

Dick Sheridan is a multi-instrumentalist who plays all the fretted string instruments: mandolin, guitar, ukulele, tenor and 5-stirng banjo. Although he does not play the fiddle, he has a great affection for the instrument and its tunes, and he enjoys playing them on all his different instruments. But apart from the fiddle itself, no other instrument quite captures the feeling of fiddle tunes than the mandolin. Unquestionably that's due to the symbiotic relationship of both instruments that share the same tuning, range, and similar voice.

Dick's association with the mandolin goes back to his early high school days. The elderly grandmother of a childhood friend had been a public school music teacher on top of whose elegant scarf-covered grand piano was a beautiful Neapolitan bowl-back mandolin placed there probably for purely decorative reasons. Dick was captivated by the looks of the instrument and asked if she would sell the instrument to him. Her answer was no, but she would trade it for help with yard work, and a deal was struck.

The instrument, which came with a slightly moth-eaten green felt case, proved to be not very playable. It was a modest instrument of unknown manufacture, yet the sound of the double strings and the visual aspects inspired Dick to search in time for another mandolin. Over the years that search provided a succession of better quality mandolins – Martins, Gibsons, Vegas, and lesser known vintage brands.

The bowl-back mandolin from a friend's grandmother was the first instrument that Dick acquired on his own, the first in a succession of a variety of instruments. For that reason he feels a strong sentimental attachment to it. He still has that "Potato Bug" mandolin, still unplayable, but still treasured. Now it proudly sits on top of Dick's upright piano, a nostalgic reminder of how his affection for the mandolin first began. That affection has continued for many years and indeed continues to this very day.

~*~

Introduction

One of the most popular of all the fretted instruments, the small mandolin packs a wallop of sound either for soloing or back-up playing. Descended from the lute family, it boasts a proud history that ranges from classical compositions by the likes of Beethoven and Vivaldi to folk music, jazz, and on to its current demand for inclusion in bluegrass and string bands.

The mandolin's unique sound is attributed to both its high pitch and the double stringing of each of its four courses or groups of strings. The slight discrepancy in pitch between the double strings produces a resonance that creates a "quivering" sound so characteristic of the instrument.

In the world of fretted string instruments, the mandolin, however, does not stand alone as a double strung instrument. Its predecessor the lute combines both single and doubled strings. The 12-string guitar doubles each of its six courses (some doubles separated by an octave). The rarely heard tiple (pronounced "tipple") not only doubles some of its strings but also includes triples. Usually consisting of 10 strings, the tiple's four courses are arranged in groups of twos and threes, such as 22-333-333-22. The instrument is sometimes incorrectly referred to as a "tripple" since its two inner courses are triply strung.

Over the years the shape of the mandolin has evolved through numerous configurations. Early mandolins with a bowled back looked much like a miniature lute. This so-called Neapolitan style with its rounded belly of alternating stripes of wood gave rise to its nickname of a "potato bug" or "tater bug" mandolin.

There have been mandolins with flat backs and tops, various body shapes, and ones with carved arched tops and bottoms. Of interest is the simple Army-Navy model made by Gibson and sold during the World War I period at military Post Exchange stores allegedly for troops as a battlefield diversion. Inexpensive and absolutely basic, it was flat as a pancake with a rounded body and a large oval-shaped sound hole.

The so-called Golden Age of the mandolin spanned the years from the early 20th century to about the 1930s. Although there were several commercial companies producing mandolins during this period, the market was unquestionably dominated by the Gibson Company. Gibson offered two styles of mandolins, the plain bodied teardrop shaped A series and the more elaborate model called the F series which featured a scroll top, scrolled peghead, and two projecting "points" sticking out from the side of the body.

Within each of these series there were upgrades designated by numbers like A1, A2, A3, A4 and F1, F2, F3, and F4. The higher the number the more ornamented the instrument.

Modifications in the F series occurred in 1922 when master craftsman and designer Lloyd Loar introduced the top level Gibson F5 mandolin. This instrument -- so coveted today by both players and collectors -- incorporated superior materials, craftsmanship, and ornamentation. Loar also extended the F5's neck and designed a "floating" fingerboard that was not glued to the instrument's body. The configuration of the sound hole was also changed from ovals to f-shapes inspired by those of a violin.

But as the century progressed, interest in the mandolin waned, giving way to other instruments like the guitar and banjo. The tide turned, however, with the appearance in the 1950s of Bill Monroe and his Blue Grass Boys. Monroe's band and his electrifying speed and virtuosity on the mandolin set the stage for the development of bluegrass music and its ever-increasing popularity -- and the resurgence of interest in the mandolin.

For most of his performing years Monroe played a high-end Gibson F5 mandolin produced in 1923 and signed by Lloyd Loar. That instrument can now be seen in Nashville at the Country Music Hall of Fame.

Bill Monroe was no stranger to fiddle music. His mother's brother Penfield ("Uncle Pen") was a fiddler who taught Bill many old-time tunes that were later performed with the Blue Grass Boys and have now become bluegrass standards. Both instruments, the fiddle and the mandolin, are today vital components of most bluegrass and old-time string bands.

The combination of fiddle and mandolin popularized by Bill Monroe is indeed a perfect union. It is responsible for sustaining interest in the vast repertoire of traditional fiddle music as well as for a dynamic renewal of interest in the mandolin. A representative sample of some of the best in fiddle music arranged for the mandolin can be found in the following pages. It offers an exciting and diverse collection– for individuals and groups alike -- while opening a world of music perhaps previously undiscovered for the mandolin and now most certainly to be enjoyed and treasured.

~*~

ANGELINE, THE BAKER

Mandolin tuning: GDAE

TRADITIONAL

ASH GROVE

Mandolin tuning: GDAE

TRADITIONAL

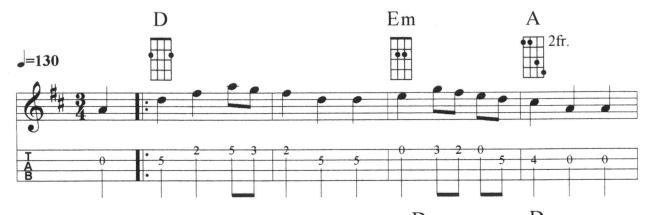

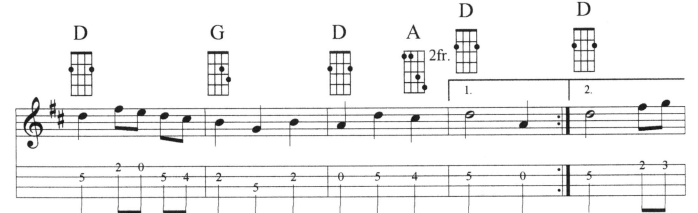

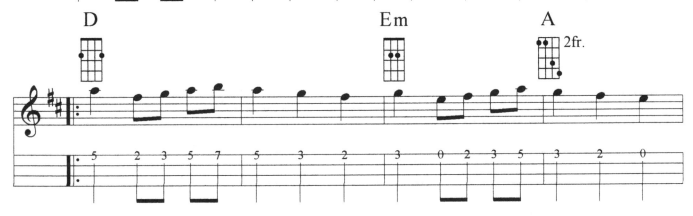

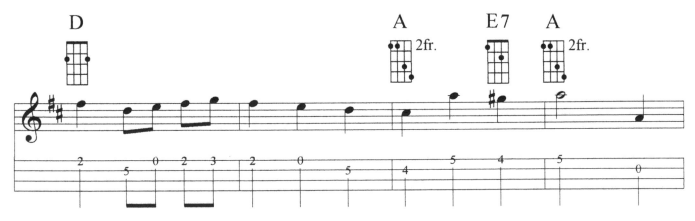

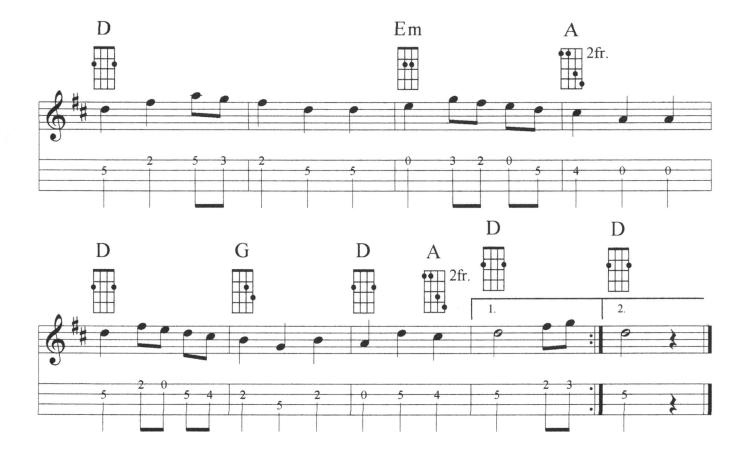

ARKANSAS TRAVELER

Mandolin tuning: GDAE

TRADITIONAL

BILLY IN THE LOWGROUND

Mandolin tuning: GDAE

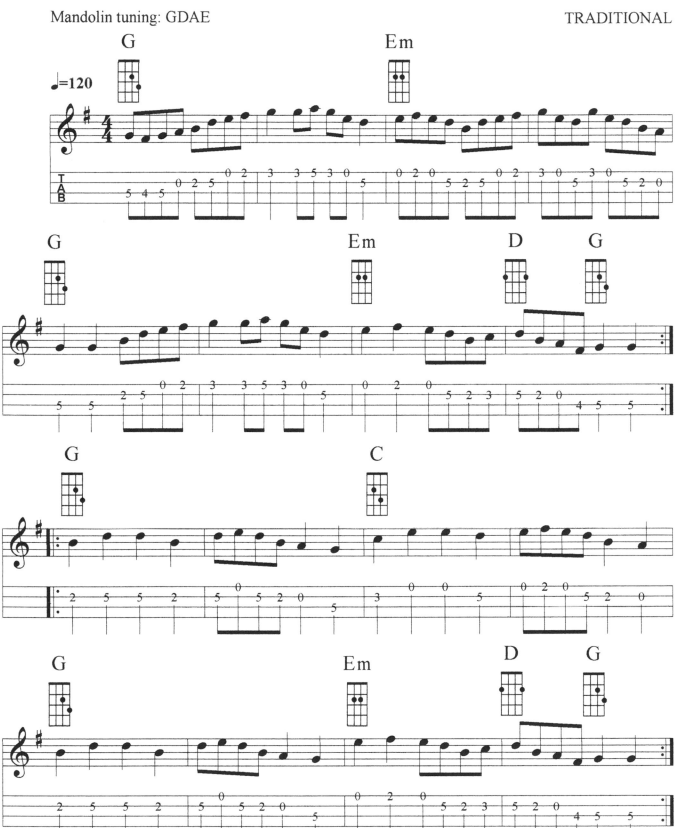

THE BOATMEN

Mandolin tuning: GDAE

TRADITIONAL

BONAPARTE'S RETREAT

Mandolin tuning: GDAE

TRADITIONAL

CHERISH THE LADIES

Mandolin tuning: GDAE

TRADITIONAL

CONSTANT BILLY

Mandolin tuning: GDAE

TRADITIONAL

COTTON-EYE JOE

Mandolin tuning: GDAE

TRADITIONAL

CRIPPLE CREEK

Mandolin tuning: GDAE

TRADITIONAL

DEVIL'S DREAM

Mandolin tuning: GDAE

TRADITIONAL

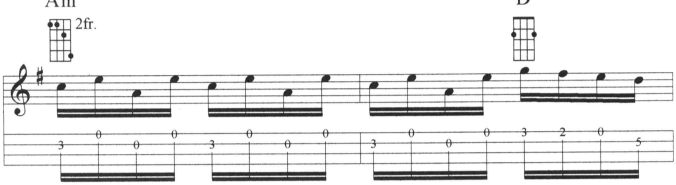

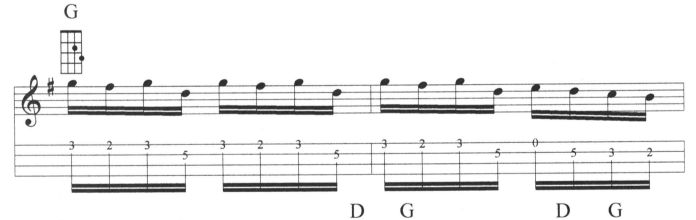

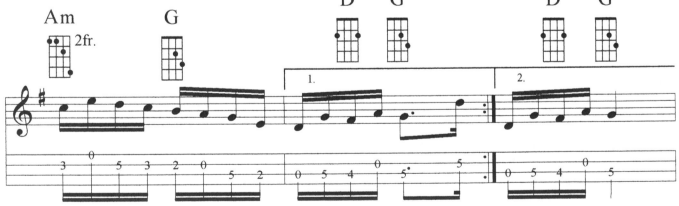

DEVIL'S DREAM

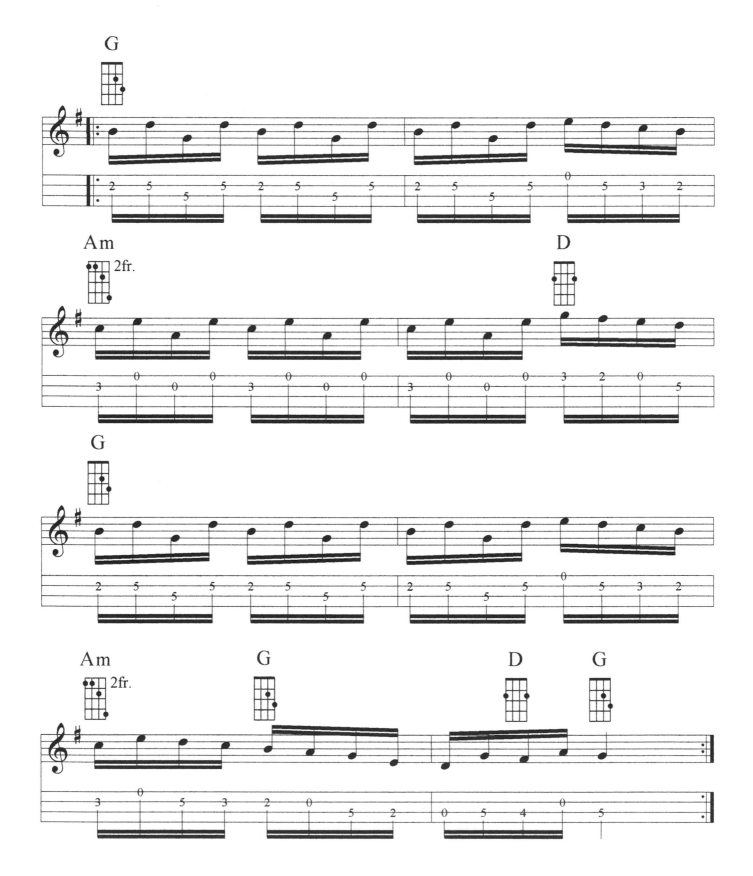

DURANG'S HORNPIPE

Mandolin tuning: GDAE

TRADITIONAL

EIGHTH OF JANUARY

Mandolin tuning: GDAE

TRADITIONAL

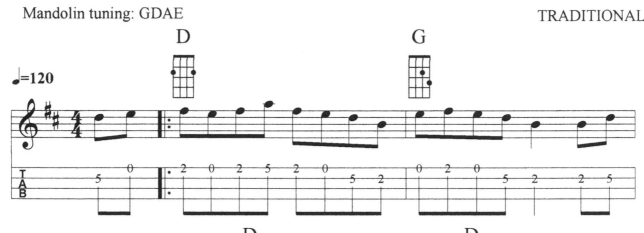

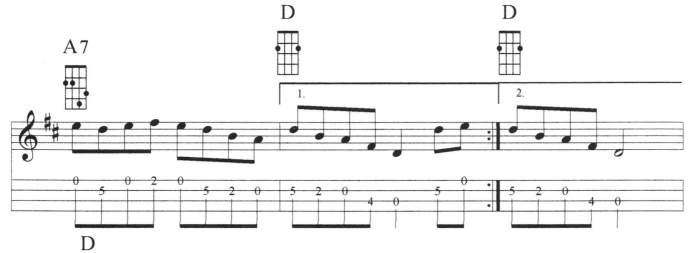

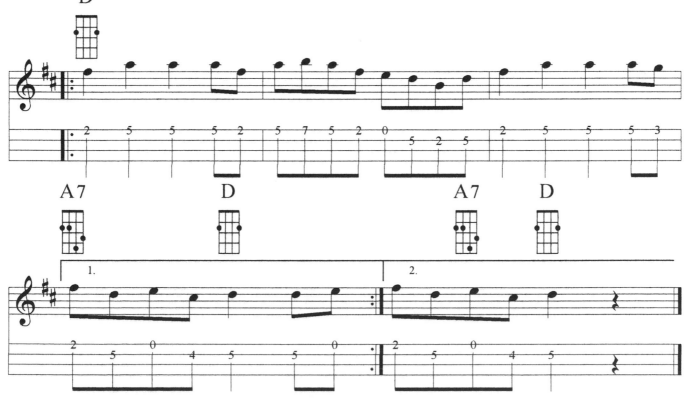

FAREWELL TO WHISKEY

Mandolin tuning: GDAE

TRADITIONAL

FISHER'S HORNPIPE

Mandolin tuning: GDAE

TRADITIONAL

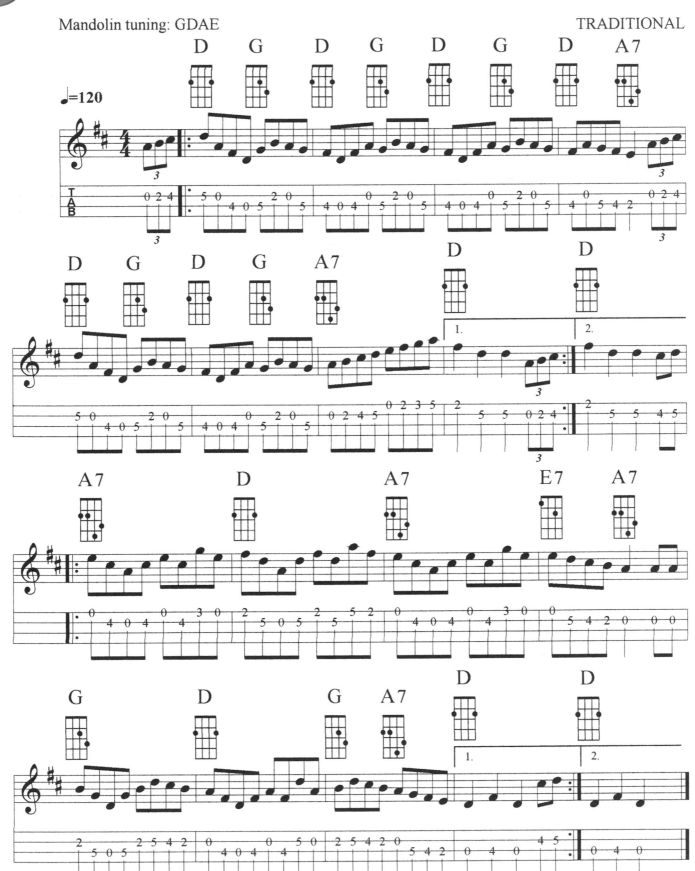

FLOP-EARED MULE

Mandolin tuning: GDAE

TRADITIONAL

FLOWERS OF EDINBURGH

Mandolin tuning: GDAE

TRADITIONAL

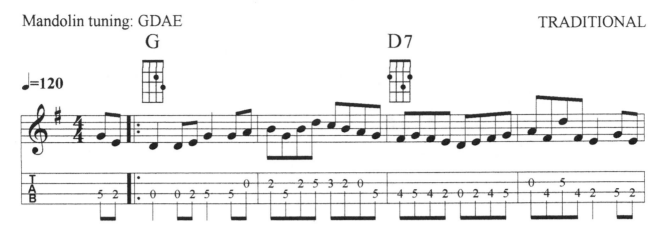

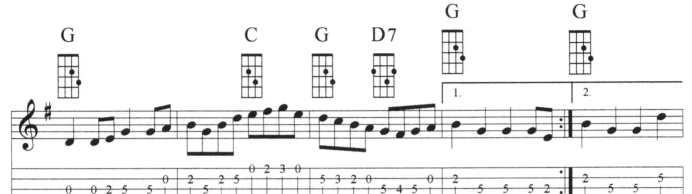

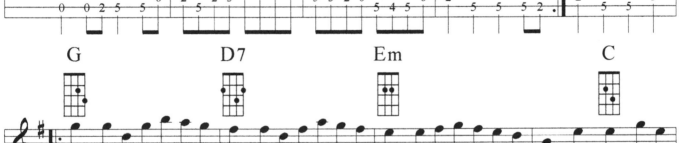

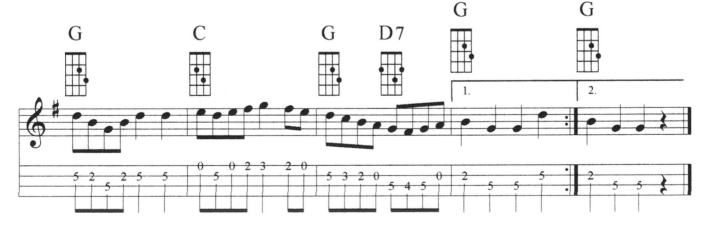

FORKED DEER

Mandolin tuning: GDAE

TRADITIONAL

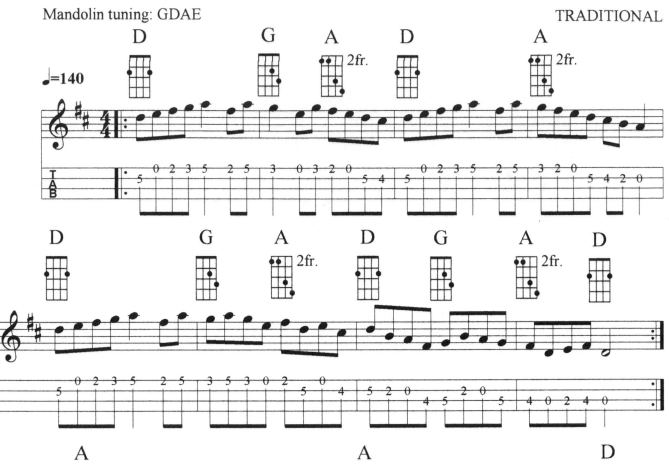

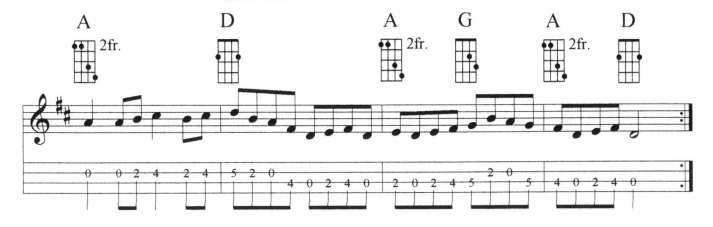

THE GIRL I LEFT BEHIND

Mandolin tuning: GDAE

TRADITIONAL

GOLDEN SLIPPERS

Mandolin tuning: GDAE

TRADITIONAL

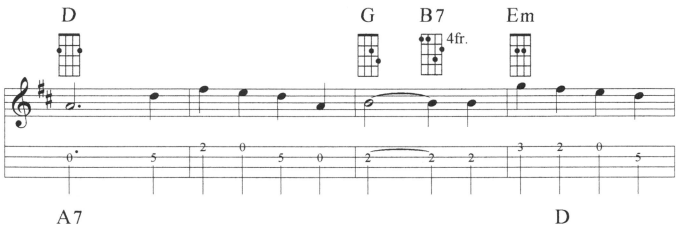

GRANDPA'S WALTZ

Mandolin tuning: GDAE

TRADITIONAL

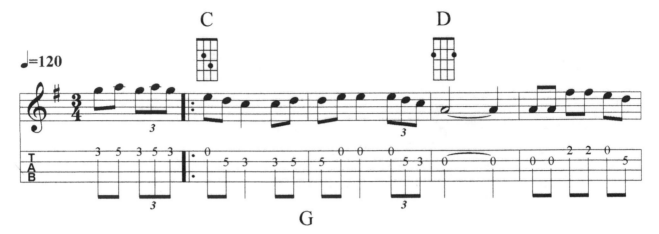

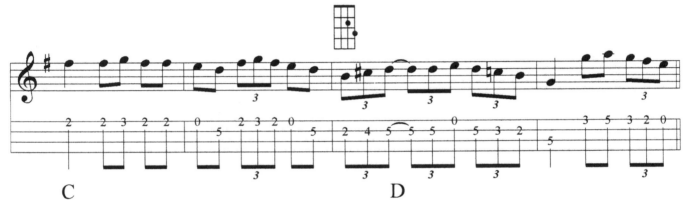

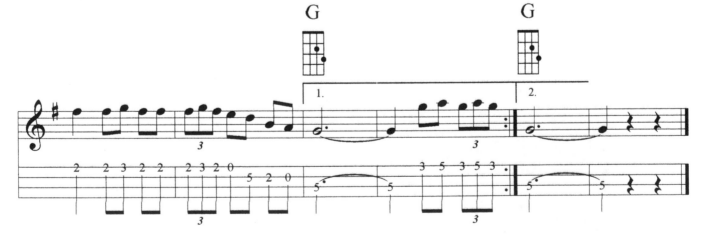

HASTE TO THE WEDDING

Mandolin tuning: GDAE

TRADITIONAL

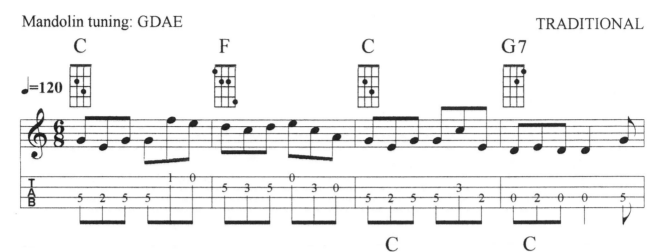

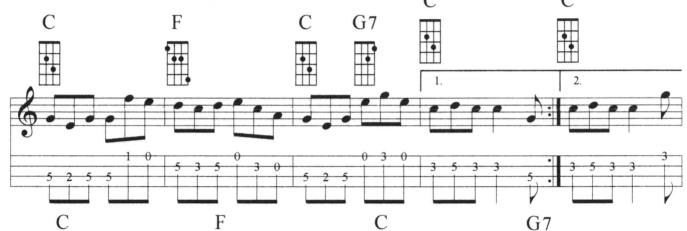

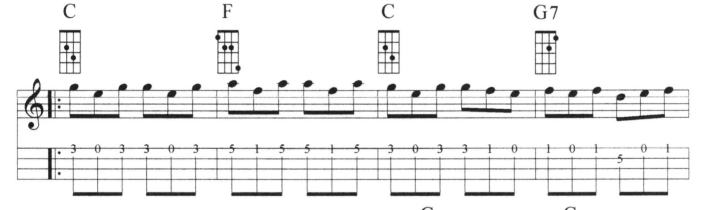

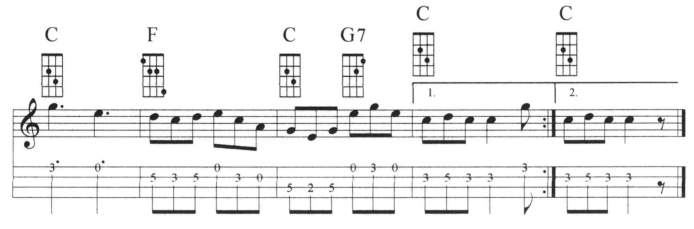

HARVEST HOME

Mandolin tuning: GDAE

TRADITIONAL

IRISH WASHERWOMAN

Mandolin tuning: GDAE

TRADITIONAL

JOHN HARDY

Mandolin tuning: GDAE

TRADITIONAL

JOLIE BLONDE

Mandolin tuning: GDAE

JOLIE BLONDE

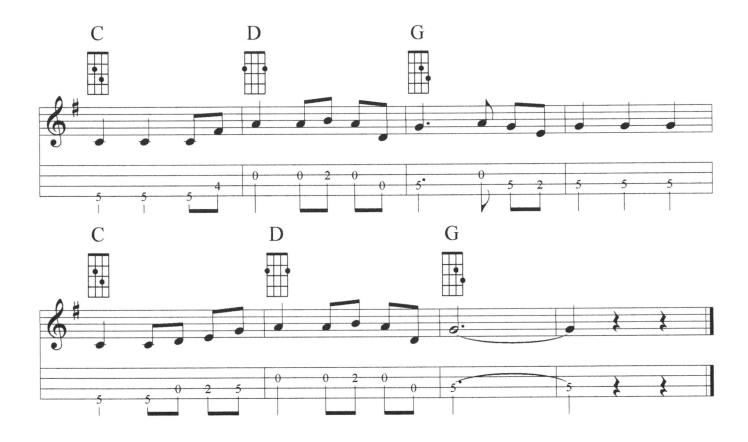

Eddie Collins

JOYS OF QUEBEC

Mandolin tuning: GDAE

TRADITIONAL

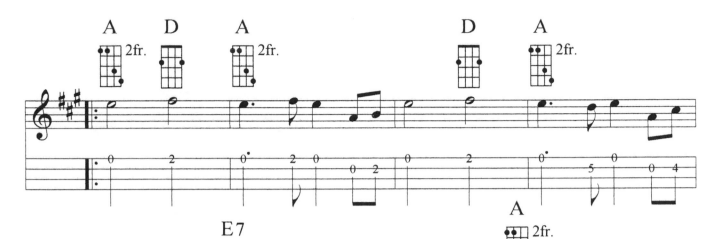

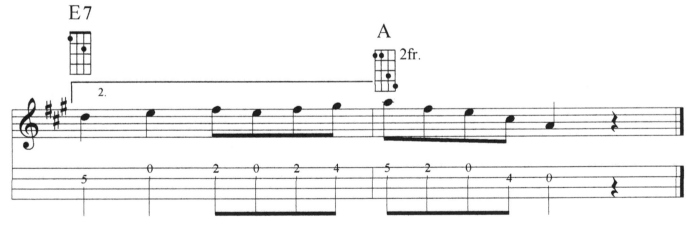

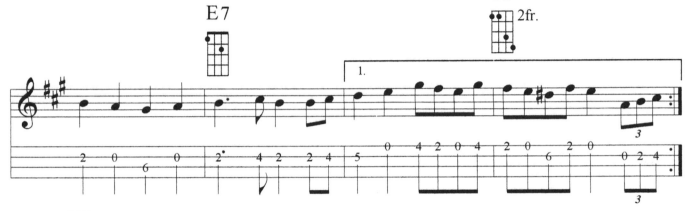

Buy a A4 Gibson Mandolin for only $3 a month… in 1915

39

LEATHER BRITCHES

Mandolin tuning GDAE

TRADITIONAL

LIBERTY

Mandolin tuning: GDAE

TRADITIONAL

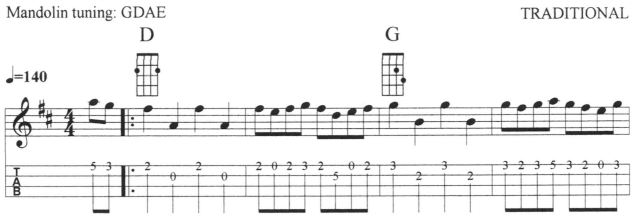

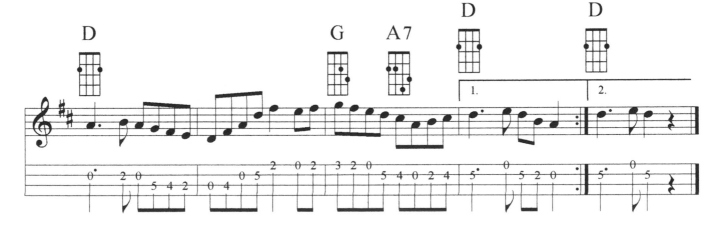

THE LITTLE OLD LOG CABIN IN THE LANE

Mandolin tuning: GDAE

TRADITIONAL

A MAIDEN'S PRAYER

Mandolin tuning: GDAE

TRADITIONAL

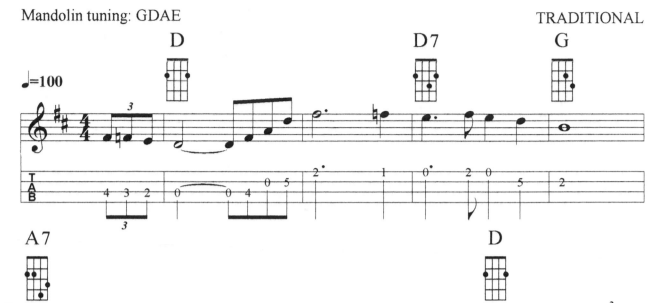

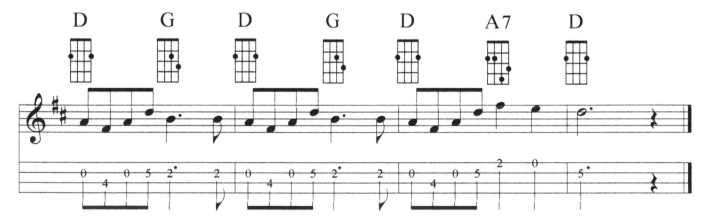

MASON'S APRON

Mandolin tuning: GDAE

TRADITIONAL

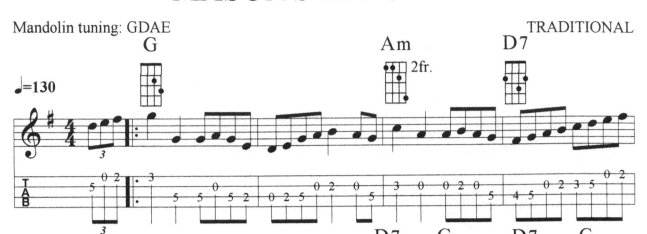

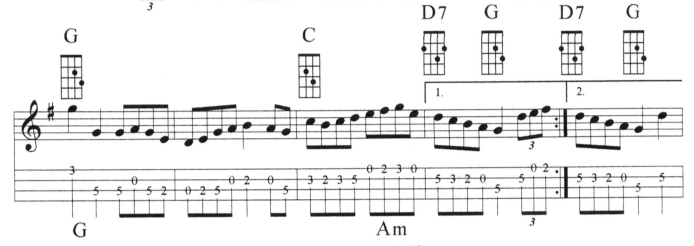

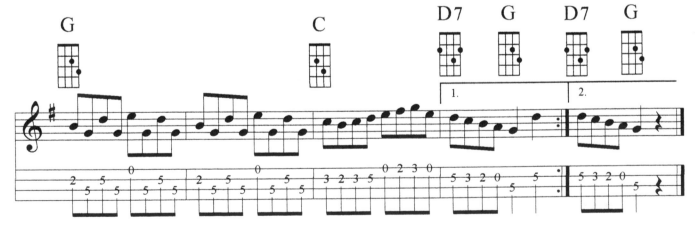

MISS McLEOD'S REEL

Mandolin tuning: GDAE

TRADITIONAL

MISSISSIPPI SAWYER

Mandolin tuning: GDAE

TRADITIONAL

OLD JOE CLARK

Mandolin tuning: GDAE

TRADITIONAL

PADDY ON THE TURNPIKE

Mandolin tuning: GDAE

TRADITIONAL

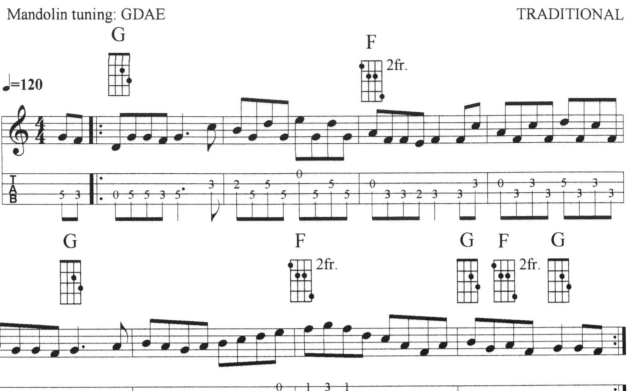

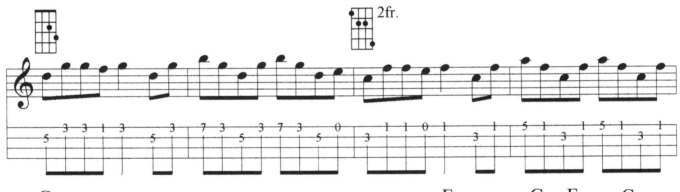

RAGTIME ANNIE

Mandolin tuning: GDAE

TRADITIONAL

RED HAIRED BOY

Mandolin tuning: GDAE

TRADITIONAL

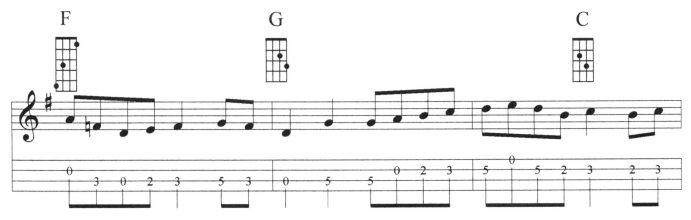

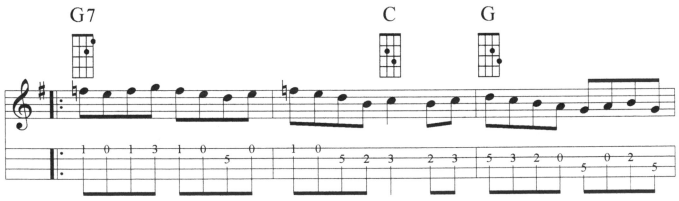

RED WING

Mandolin tuning: GDAE

Lyrics by: THURLAND CHATTAWAY

Music by: KERRY MILLS

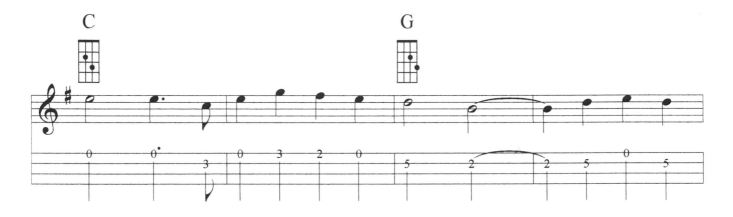

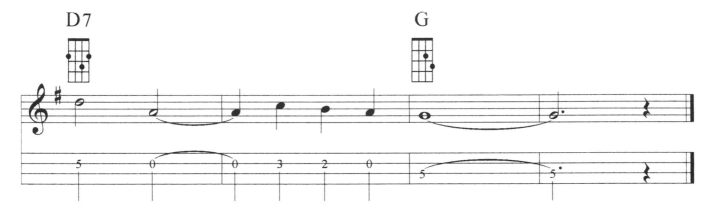

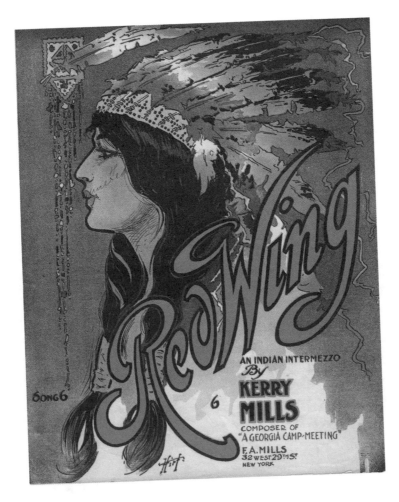

SAILOR'S HORNPIPE

Mandolin tuning: GDAE

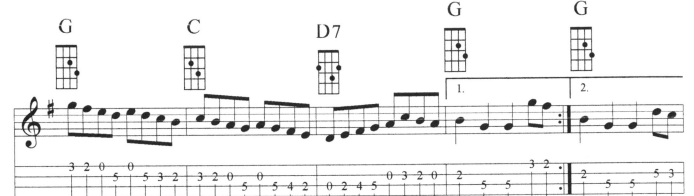

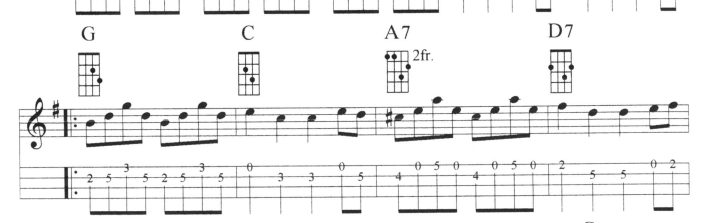

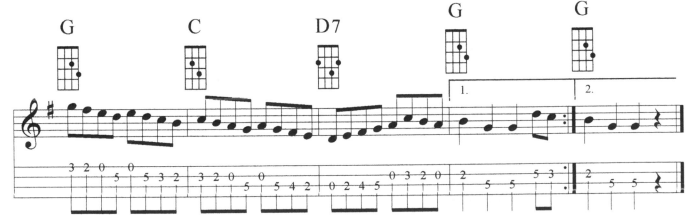

54

SALLY GOODIN

Mandolin tuning: GDAE

TRADITIONAL

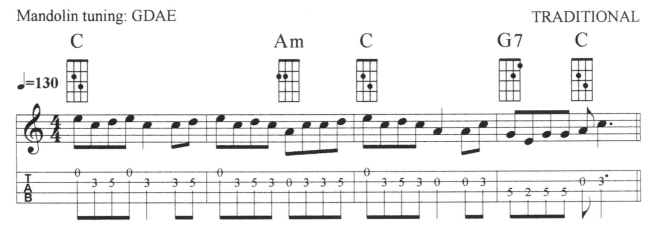

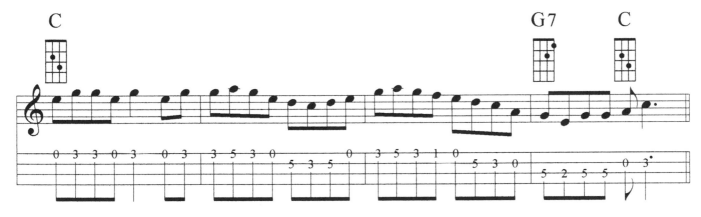

Mandolin tuning: GDAE

TRADITIONAL

SCOTLAND THE BRAVE

Mandolin tuning: GDAE

TRADITIONAL

♩=120

SNOW DEER

Mandolin tuning: GDAE

TRADITIONAL

SOLDIER'S JOY

Mandolin tuning: GDAE

TRADITIONAL

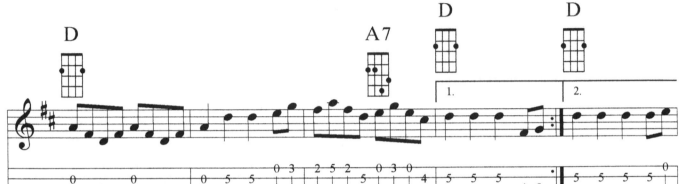

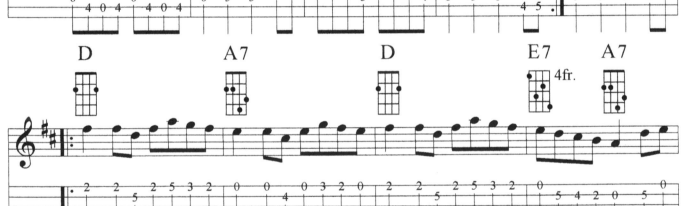

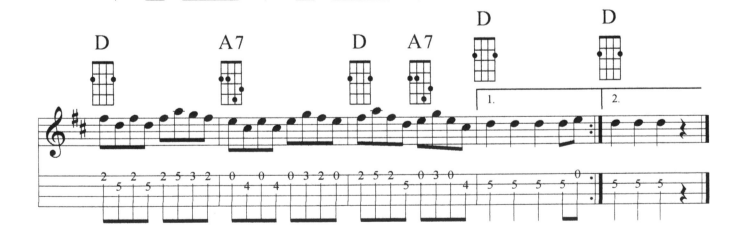

ST. ANNE'S REEL

Mandolin tuning: GDAE

TRADITIONAL

TEMPERANCE REEL

Mandolin tuning: GDAE

TRADITIONAL

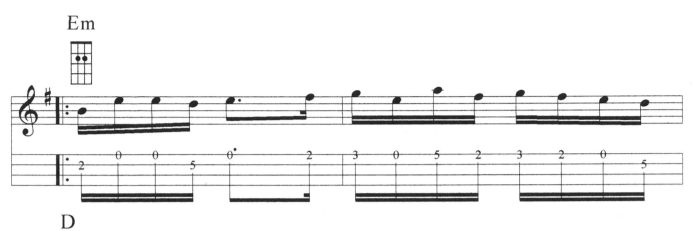

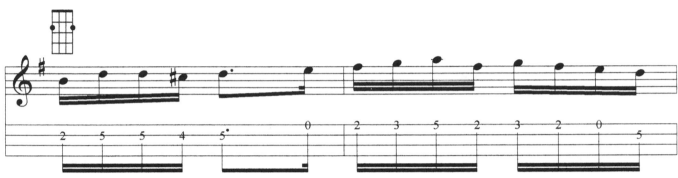

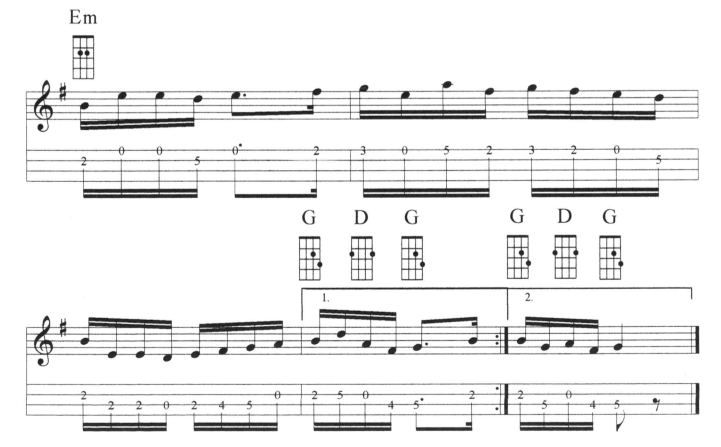

TURKEY IN THE STRAW

Mandolin tuning: GDAE

TRADITIONAL

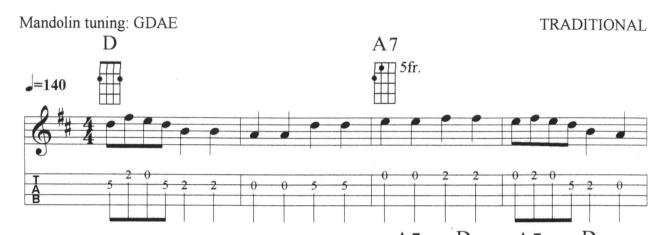

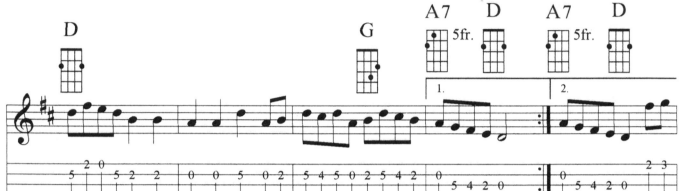

UP JUMPED THE DEVIL
(Similar to "Ragtime Annie")

Mandolin tuning: GDAE

TRADITIONAL

WHISKEY BEFORE BREAKFAST

Mandolin tuning: GDAE

TRADITIONAL

More Great Books from Dick Sheridan...

More Great Mandolin Books from Centerstream...

MANDOLIN CHORDS PLUS
TAB

by Ron Middlebrook

Features chords, scales, tunings, hot licks and songs. Shows over 300 chord fingerings, 18 hot licks used for intros, endings and turn-arounds, how to read tablature, several scales and 2 songs..

00000040 ....$3.75

MANDOLIN CHRISTMAS
TAB

arr. Eric Cutshall

18 favorites, each presented in two versions: a simple lead sheet arrangment with melody, lyrics and chords; and an advanced solo arrangement that combines the melody and accompaniment. Includes: Adeste Fideles • Deck the Halls • The First Noel • Good King Wenceslas • Jingle Bells • and more.

00001209 Softcover...9.95

ASAP BLUEGRASS MANDOLIN
TAB

Learn How to Play the Bluegrass Way
by Eddie Collins

This book/2-CD pack delivers the meat and potatoes of bluegrass mandolin way beyond just teaching fiddle tunes! Players will discover how to find their way around the neck using common double stops, develop creative back-up skills, play solos to vocal tunes in the style of Bill Monroe, make up their own solos, and a whole lot more. For the average learner, this pack represents nearly two years worth of lessons! Includes two (2) instructional CDs: one plays every example in the book, and the 2nd contains 32 songs performed by a bluegrass band with the mandolin parts separated on the right channel.

00001219 Book/2-CD Pack $24.95

ASAP IRISH MANDOLIN
TAB

by Doc Rossi

Doc Rossi, a well-known musician in both traditional and early music, has created this book for mandolin players who want to improve their technique, develop ideas and learn new repertoire ASAP.

The tunes in this book have been arranged by genre and in order of difficulty. Starting with the basics of ornamentation in traditional Irish music, Doc then goes directly into the tunes, in tablature and standard notation. Right-hand and left-hand techniques, ornamentation and other topics are taught through the tunes themselves.

00128349 Book/CD Pack $19.99

OLD TIME STRING BAND MUSIC FOR MANDOLIN
TAB

by Joe Weidlich

70 Old Time Music Period Songs. Many of the songs recorded by string band artists in the 1920s and early 1930s were often rearrangements, in the truest folk tradition, of songs learned from a local community's oral tradition or "borrowed" from existing published song collections, child ballads, hymn books, historical events, etc., using new words and/or titles for a particular song. Pick up your mandolin and start having fun!

00128131 Book/CD Pack $19.99

P.O. Box 17878 - Anaheim Hills, CA 92817
(714) 779-9390   www.centerstream-usa.com